W9-ANR-334

The Oceans

Rain Forest, Borneo

Rain Forest, New Guinea

Lahore,
Pakistan

New Zealand

Mount Everest

The Serengeti

The Mallee, Australia

Paradise whydah

EXOTIC BIRDS

By Marilyn Singer

Illustrated by James Needham

Doubleday

NEW YORK LONDON TORONTO SYDNEY AUCKLAND

Published by Doubleday,
a division of Bantam Doubleday Dell
Publishing Group, Inc.
666 Fifth Avenue, New York, New York
10103
Doubleday
and the portrayal of an anchor with a
dolphin
are trademarks of Doubleday,
a division of Bantam Doubleday Dell
Publishing Group, Inc.
Library of Congress Cataloging-in-
Publication Data
Singer, Marilyn.
    Exotic birds/by Marilyn Singer;
illustrated by James Needham.
       p. cm.
    Summary: Introduces the
characteristics of such exotic birds as
the Galápagos penguin, kiwi, and
African hornbill.
    1. Birds—Juvenile literature. [1.
Birds.] I. Needham, James, ill. II.
Title.
QL676.2.S57 1990
    598—dc20 89-35691 CIP AC
R.L. 3.6
ISBN 0-385-26571-9
ISBN 0-385-26572-7 (lib. bdg.)
Text copyright © 1990 by Marilyn
Singer
Illustrations copyright © 1990 by James
Needham

All Rights Reserved
Printed in Italy
February 1991
First Edition

Introduction

You are walking through a jungle in South America. High up in a tree you see a monkey swinging by its tail. A shadow passes overhead. Zap! Before you can blink, sharp claws grab the monkey and carry it away. You have just seen a harpy eagle getting its dinner. . . .

It is a hot, dry day. Your jeep is moving slowly through the African plain. Up the road watching you is a tall, long-necked figure standing on two scaly legs. You drive a little closer, and, whoosh, off it goes, dashing across the brown grass at forty-five miles per hour. Quick, snap a picture! It's an ostrich on the run. . . .

You have been in cold places before, but no place is as cold as this. It's a good thing you're only visiting. Who or what, you ask, could live at seventy-five degrees below zero? Then you see them, thousands of them, huddled together, each with an egg on his foot. What are they? Emperor penguins, spending the whole winter in a world of ice. . . .

Harpy eagle, ostrich, emperor penguin. What do all of these strange creatures have in common? They are birds—exotic birds.

What makes a bird a bird? In a word —*feathers.* All birds—and only birds— have feathers. They have feathers for four main reasons: 1) to keep themselves warm; 2) to keep themselves dry; 3) to disguise themselves from enemies or to advertise themselves to possible mates, friends, or rivals; 4) to fly. The number of feathers each bird has varies from species to species. A little ruby-throated hummingbird has more than nine hundred. A large whistling swan has over twenty-five thousand. Various types of birds shed their feathers once or twice (or, more rarely, three times) a year. This process is called *molting.* The molting is generally gradual. The feathers are shed and replaced a few at a time over a number of weeks, months, or even years. The plumage of some birds, usually the males of the species, changes dramatically during the mating season. It becomes more colorful, decorative, or both. When the season is over, the "fancy dress" is molted.

Because feathers are essential to their survival, birds spend a lot of time caring for them. They keep them free of dirt, insects, and germs, and pull out broken or frayed feathers to allow new ones to replace them. Some birds take baths in water to keep clean. Others use sand or dust. Birds also use their beaks to clean and fluff their feathers and to smear oil from special glands, or a unique powder from powder-down feathers, all over themselves. This is called *preening.* It too helps keep the plumage in good shape.

Without healthy plumage, birds would have a hard time flying. Feathers —and, of course, wings—enable a bird to fly. They streamline the birds, creating smooth outer surfaces and reducing friction. Other features also help birds fly. For one thing, most birds have hollow bones. For another, they have, besides their lungs, a system of bubblelike air sacs throughout their bodies. This allows them to use air more efficiently than most other

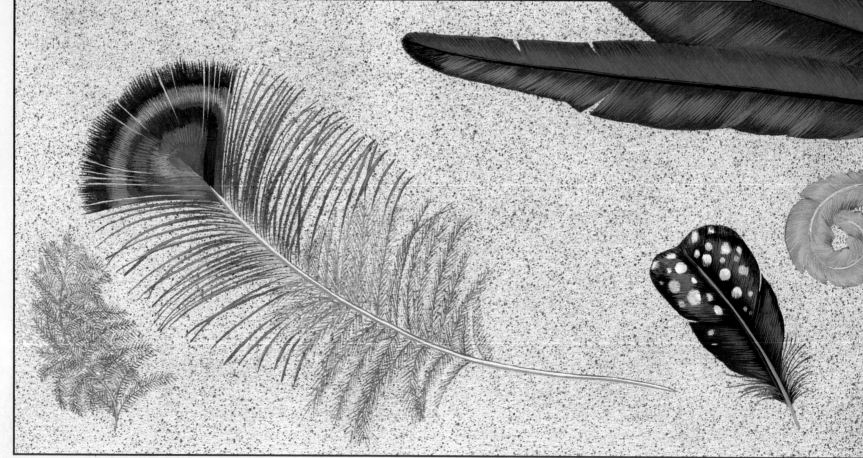

animals. The air sacs also help keep their body temperatures low so that birds don't overheat. Good eyesight is also important to flight, and few animals can match most birds' sharp vision. A hawk soaring high up in the clouds can spot a tiny mouse on the ground one mile below.

We associate birds with flight, but the truth is that not all birds can fly. Ostriches, rheas, emus, cassowaries, kiwis, penguins, and other birds are flightless. They have undeveloped, useless wings or wings that have become flippers. Their tails are often stubby or they have no tails at all. However, most birds do fly. Some are awkward—they fly only to escape and cannot keep it up for long. Others, for example hawks, eagles, vultures, and albatrosses, with their long or broad wings and rudderlike tails, are graceful endurance flyers. Quite a number of birds travel very far by wing. They *migrate*, sometimes thousands of miles.

Migration takes place so that birds can escape dangerously cold weather and also have a constant food supply. For example, an insect-eating swallow must leave the north by the end of summer, when the bugs disappear, and head for the south, where the supply is ample.

Besides feathers and flight, we associate birds with eggs. All birds lay eggs. Birds' eggs come in many colors. They range in size from a tiny hummingbird's (.025 ounce) to a huge ostrich's (3.5 pounds). In order to hatch, eggs must be kept warm through *incubation.* One or both parents (or sometimes foster parents) incubate the eggs. They do this generally—but not always—by sitting on them. The number of eggs a bird lays may be as few as one or as many as twenty, again depending on the species. A baby bird chips out of its shell with an *egg tooth.* This tooth is a hard point on the top of its beak, which it eventually loses. Some birds are born blind, naked, and helpless. Others, such as baby chickens and ducks, are covered with fluffy feathers called *down.* They are ready to walk or swim a few hours after hatching.

A female bird must, of course, have a place to lay her eggs. We usually think of her and her mate building a nest. But just as not all birds fly, not all build nests either. Some lay eggs in holes in trees, cliffs, or riverbanks or in underground tunnels. Some scratch out a shallow trough in the earth. Poorwills and other nightjars don't even bother with a trough. They lay their well-camouflaged eggs right on the flat ground. However, most birds are nest builders. Their nests differ greatly in size, shape, and design—from the sloppy collection of twigs a pigeon tosses together to the complex communal structure of the sociable weaver. Nests are made of twigs, branches, feathers, leaves, twine, paper, and many other materials. Birds may cement the materials together with mud or saliva. The smallest nests, those of the hummingbirds, are only an inch in diameter. The largest, the scrub fowls' mound nests made of leaves, may be ten or more yards wide.

Beaks are another distinctive bird feature. They are lighter than teeth, which makes flight easier, and they are often quite flexible. They may be daggerlike, spearlike, upturned, downturned, hooked, flat, shaped like a shoe or like a spoon. The shape of a bird's bill usually indicates its diet. Birds of prey have hooked beaks for tearing meat. Parrots have strong curved ones for cracking nuts. The long, pointed bills of anhingas are designed to spear fish. Different birds have different diets. Some are restricted to a few types of food. Others eat

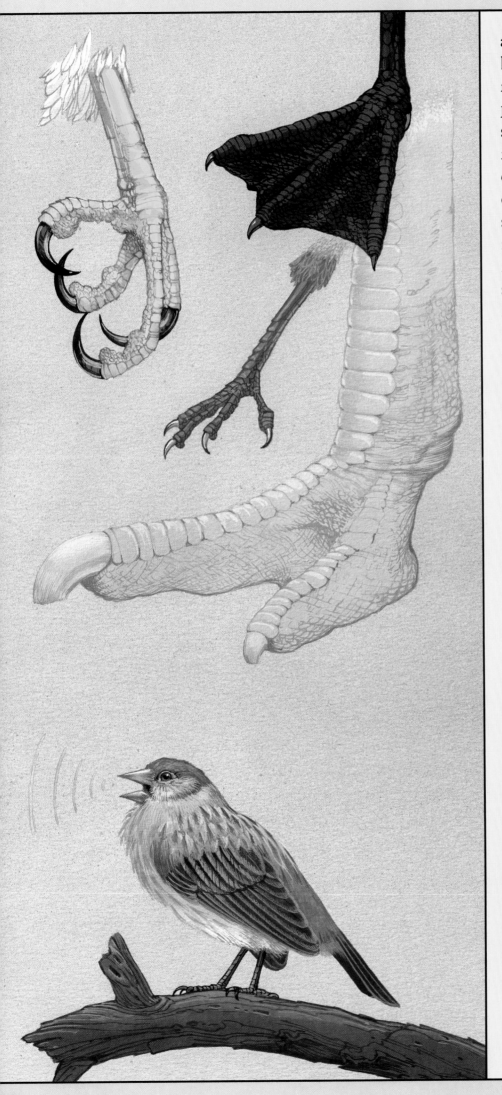

almost anything. Among the things birds eat are insects, seeds, fruit, nectar, roots, tubers, grass, buds, pollen, sap, plankton, fish, rodents, mammals, snakes, lizards, frogs, carrion (the remains of dead animals), eggs, and other birds. Because birds use so much energy, they need to eat a lot. The old saying that he or she "eats like a bird," meaning the person doesn't eat much, is totally wrong. In proportion to their size, birds are among the biggest eaters in the world.

Birds' feet also tell something about their diets and a lot about their lifestyles and habitats. Most birds have four toes on each foot. In water birds, these toes are webbed for swimming. But flightless running birds may have fewer toes. The ostrich has only two. Birds of prey have sharp claws, or *talons,* to catch their food. Perching birds have a built-in locking device in their feet that pulls their toes into a fist. That way a bird can sleep without falling off a branch.

One final thing that distinguishes birds is their voices. Birds use their voices to communicate with mates, enemies, friends, and their young. Their calls announce food, danger, the desire to mate, and many other things. In addition to calls or sounds, some birds are famous for their songs. However, they do not sing for the joy of it—or at least not mostly for that. They usually sing to mark territory and to attract mates. They may also dance, posture, display plumage, clack beaks, and present gifts. Some of these techniques, along with other behavior, are what make many birds so fascinatingly odd.

Now let's take a tour and get a closer look at some of the world's most odd and exotic birds.

The Pribilof Islands

A cold, wet, and rocky island almost three hundred miles from Alaska in the middle of the Bering Sea may not seem like a place to see a lot of birds. But in the breeding season the cliffs of St. Paul Island of the Pribilof island group look like enormous open-air apartment houses—summer homes for over one million arctic birds.

Among the birds on St. Paul's ledges are great colonies of *kittiwakes* and *murres*. Kittiwakes are gulls. They build nests of seaweed, grass, and mud and cement them to the ledges. Often the nests overlap the edges. The height and dangerous location of their nests keep the birds safe from *predators*—animals that eat them. But if the eggs or the young were to fall, they'd be instantly crushed. So, not only do the adults sit quietly on their nests, but, unlike other baby gulls, kittiwake chicks stay put. They barely move until they can fly away.

Murres do not build nests at all. Each female murre lays one tear-shaped egg on the bare ledge. Some *ornithologists*—

Common murre

Red-legged kittiwake

Tufted puffin

Horned puffin

scientists who study birds—say the shape allows the egg to roll in a circle, so it won't tumble off the cliff. Baby murres leave the ledge before they can fly. Their parents give a special "leaping" call and the young plunge off the cliffs, sometimes hundreds of feet, to the water below.

Murres are in the *auk,* or *alcid,* family. Perhaps the most famous and well-loved auks are the *puffins,* with their plump bodies and colorful oversized bills. Two types of puffins nest on St. Paul. The *horned puffin* has a small "horn" it can raise above each eye. The *tufted puffin* is named for the long pale plumes on either side of its head. In the fall the birds molt these horns and tufts, along with the colorful outer sheath of their beaks. Both horned and tufted puffins use their sharp claws to dig burrows in the soft earth at the top of the cliffs. Like the murres and the kittiwakes, they will spend only a short time on land to raise their young. The rest of the year is spent on the open sea.

In the past, puffins were killed by people for food. Today, although they are sometimes still hunted, puffins—and many other arctic birds—are in greater danger from oil spills.

The Atlantic Coast

If you walk along any of the beaches on the coast of Eastern North America at any time of year, you are bound to see many different kinds of birds. Some, like gulls and terns, will be flying over the ocean. Others will be on the shore, probing at the water's edge for food. Among these shorebirds you might spot the *American oystercatcher.*

From its name, you might guess that an oystercatcher eats oysters—and you'd be right. However, the oystercatcher also feeds on worms, crabs, and other mollusks besides oysters. The bird has the unique ability to open mollusk shells with its long, flat, chisel-like bill, which it hammers or stabs between the two halves of the shell.

On or over the ocean you will often see diving birds called *cormorants.* To catch fish, cormorants can plunge seventy to one hundred feet under the water, although they usually make shallower dives. One thing that may allow cormorants to dive so deep is the lack of oil or waterproofing on their wing feathers. But because they lack waterproofing, cormorants must dry

Osprey

American oystercatcher

Double-crested cormorant

Black skimmer

their wings in the sun. That's why you will often see the birds perched on rocks, buoys, and sandbars with their wings outstretched.

A very different diver is the *osprey*—North America's only fish-eating hawk. From the sky the osprey scans the water. When it spots its prey, the bird plummets down feet first to snatch up the fish, which may be heavier than the bird itself. One of the osprey's three front toes is reversible so that it can be used as a hind toe to grasp the slippery prey. Although when fishing the osprey may submerge completely, it does not dive far below the water's surface.

A fish-eater with a special technique is the *black skimmer.* The skimmer is the only bird whose *lower mandible*—the lower half of the beak—is longer than the upper. The skimmer flies low over the ocean, plowing the water with its beak. When the lower mandible strikes a fish, the upper one snaps down to trap it. One other unique feature of the skimmer is the vertical pupils of its eyes, which, like a cat's, can be narrowed to slits. This feature helps reduce sun glare and also lets the skimmer fish at night—something other shorebirds generally do not do.

The Sonoran Desert

A desert is not an easy place in which to live. Hot and dry much of the year and sometimes bitter cold the rest, a desert is home to a unique group of plants and animals that have adapted to withstand the extremes of temperature and lack of water. In Arizona's Sonoran Desert the most familiar plants are the cacti. The most spectacular of these is the *saguaro*. The saguaro is the world's largest cactus. It can rise as high as forty feet. It provides food and sometimes shelter for many desert animals, especially birds.

Gila woodpeckers use strong claws and stiff tails to climb the saguaros. They probe for insects with their stout bills and long, sticky, bristle-tipped tongues. These woodpeckers also chisel out nesting holes in the cacti. During the day the temperature inside these holes may be as much as twenty degrees cooler than the temperature outside. At night, when the temperature drops, the holes stay warm and snug.

Gila woodpecker

Greater roadrunner

Elf owl

Western poorwill

Gila woodpeckers use these sites for one season only. In subsequent seasons they may be taken over by other birds such as martins, finches, flycatchers, and even a type of owl. No bigger than a sparrow and the smallest of all owls, the *elf owl* never digs a nest. It uses the holes dug by gila and other woodpeckers in cacti or in desert trees and bushes. Like most other owls, it hunts at night, eating mostly insects, scorpions, and spiders. It is a fairly common desert bird but is seldom seen in the daytime.

The *poorwill* is another desert bird that hunts at night. It is also the only bird that *hibernates.* During the cold Sonoran winters the poorwill's body temperature drops nearly forty degrees to about 65° F. Its breathing slows to almost nothing, and it stops digesting food. It may stay in this state for three months or so, until spring.

No visit to the Sonoran Desert would be complete without a glimpse at that famous sprinter—the *roadrunner.* This bird can run fifteen to twenty miles per hour. It can also swerve into a turn in an instant and make fast stops, using its tail as a brake or rudder. A day hunter, the roadrunner eats many things, including snakes. It can actually kill a rattler with its sharp beak.

The Everglades

"Pa-hay-okee," the River of Grass. That is what Native Americans called the Everglades, the area of sawgrass marshes dotted with clumps of palms, dense mangrove patches, and dark cypress swamps in southern Florida. It is now a national park.

Food is plentiful as long as the water level is high, so alligators, snakes, several mammals, and many birds feed and breed here. In the winter especially, you are likely to see a lot of birds, particularly the long-billed, long-legged waders such as *herons, egrets,* and *ibises.*

Among the many herons in the Everglades are the *little blue* and *green herons.* The little blue heron spends the first part of its life as a pure white bird. Then, as it grows older, its feathers slowly change until it is a pure slate blue. The green heron does not have a white phase. But it does have the fascinating habit of placing a small feather, worm, or insect on the water as a lure to catch fish.

The beautiful egrets are related to the herons. The *snowy* and *common egrets* were once killed by the thousands for their long plumes, used on women's hats and dresses. But the birds are now protected by law. Ibises are an old breed dating back some sixty million

Common egret

Snowy egret

Limpkin

Green heron

Little blue heron

American white pelican

Snail kite

Brown pelican

Glossy ibis

White ibis

Roseate spoonbill

years. Like all ibises, Florida's *white* and *glossy ibises* hunt by touch, probing in the mud with long, down-curved bills. The *roseate spoonbill,* a relative of the ibises, is also a touch feeder. It swings its spoon-shaped bill from side to side, sifting through the water for its prey.

A different kind of Everglades bird is the easily recognized *pelican.* Contrary to what you might think, pelicans do not use their large pouches to carry fish. Instead, they use them as scoops to catch prey. Their pouches squeeze out the water so that the birds can then swallow the fish. *Brown pelicans* are the only diving pelicans. They cruise above the water, then plunge down, stunning their prey with the impact. *White pelicans* fish on the water in a group.

Two rare Everglades birds are the *snail kite,* or *Everglade kite,* and the *limpkin.* The snail kite's diet consists of just one food—the apple snail. Its narrow, hooked beak is designed for picking the snail out of its shell. The limpkin, a wading bird, also depends on the apple snail, although it will take other food as well. Because of the draining and filling in of big chunks of the Everglades, as well as the mismanagement of water, this type of snail has declined. With it so have the snail kite and the limpkin. With improved land and water management programs, the birds are making a gradual comeback. But they are still very much endangered—as is the whole fragile environment of the Everglades.

A Rain Forest, Peru

Dense, dark, and drenched by up to four hundred inches of rain per year, rain forests are home to at least half of all the animal species in the world. Amazonian rain forests alone, through which flows South America's great Amazon River system, support over six hundred types of birds. So many animals can live in these jungles because food and nesting space are abundant. But sadly, the forests themselves are becoming scarce as people cut them down for wood or to make grazing land. This situation is causing worldwide concern.

The thick vegetation of the rain forests consists of a rich variety of evergreen trees, vines, ferns, orchids, and other plants. Some of the birds and other animals live in the shadowy lower and middle levels of the trees. Others inhabit the *canopy,* the sunlit upper level.

Among the common ground dwellers of this Peruvian rain forest are several kinds of *antbirds* and *manakins.* Antbirds follow columns of army ants to snatch up the bugs and animals the ants flush out as they march. Manakins perform their acrobatic courtship

Harpy eagle

Hoatzin

Golden-hooded manakin

White-bellied antbird

Yellow-crowned Amazon

Scarlet macaw

Yellow-ridged toucan

displays in arenas on the forest floor or in the lower tree branches.

Also living in the lower level is one of the world's strangest and most primitive birds—the hoatzin. Like its ancestor *archaeopteryx,* the first bird, the hoatzin is born with claws on its wings. It can crawl and hang from branches. When threatened, baby hoatzins have the unique habit of diving into the water from their nests, which overhang ponds and streams, and swimming away. When the chicks grow up, they lose their claws and their ability to dive and swim.

Way up in the canopy are the more familiar *parrots,* such as the *yellow-crowned Amazon* and several *macaws,* and the *toucans.* Parrots are colorful, largely vegetarian birds. They have powerful grasping claws and beaks, both of which they use to climb tall trees. Their beaks also have great crushing force, used to crack hard nutshells. Toucans' extra-large, brightly colored bills look heavy but are in fact quite light.

A little-known and rare canopy bird is the *harpy eagle,* the largest and probably most powerful eagle in the world. With wings measuring five and a half to seven feet long, and with feet each the size of a man's hand, this bird of prey is capable of killing monkeys and other large mammals. The destruction of rain forests has made the harpy eagle one of today's most endangered birds.

The Galápagos Islands

Imagine a group of islands where jungles are surrounded by deserts of lava and ash, where volcanoes still erupt, where strange lizards, giant tortoises, and a variety of unusual birds roam. Such a place really exists six hundred miles off the coast of Ecuador. It is called the Galápagos.

On remote, isolated groups of islands like these, birds adapt in ways different from those of their mainland relatives. The great naturalist Charles Darwin recognized this when he visited the Galápagos in 1835. Studying a group of finches there, Darwin came up with part of his theory of evolution.

One finch that he studied is the *woodpecker finch.* There are no woodpeckers on the Galápagos, and Darwin saw that this finch adapted to fill their place. The bird has a stout beak with which to bore into tree trunks and branches. But it doesn't have the woodpecker's long tongue. To make up for that, the finch has learned to use a tool to get its prey. It breaks off and shapes twigs or cactus spines and uses them to pry out insects from under the wood.

Because fresh water is scarce on the Galápagos, some of the birds that live there have developed odd drinking

Sharp-billed ground finch

Woodpecker finch

Galápagos mockingbird

Galápagos cormorant

Blue-footed booby

habits. Another of Darwin's finches, the *sharp-billed ground finch,* is one of them. It will peck holes in the skin of other birds and drink their blood. A fellow vampire is the *Galápagos mockingbird.* A superb mimic that can reproduce exactly the songs of many other birds, this mocker is a very successful island inhabitant because it will eat and drink almost anything. A mocker's meal may consist of such treats as rotten eggs, butter, carrion, vinegar, and sea lion droppings.

Another characteristic of some island-dwelling birds is flightlessness. On the Galápagos and other islands, there are few natural predators from which to escape. So some birds have become flightless. One of these is the

Galápagos cormorant. It does have wings, but they are very small and used mostly to shade its young from the sun. In the water the bird propels itself by its feet and not its wings.

A bird that flies extremely well, the *blue-footed booby* is found in other parts of the world besides the Galápagos. Tame and friendly like many island residents, the booby is a great diver. It is capable of plunging from one hundred feet in the air into a school of fish at one hundred miles per hour. Blue-footed boobies perform an entertaining courtship ritual called *parading,* during which they march around to show one another their startlingly blue feet.

The Andes

Down the western edge of South America stretches the longest mountain range in the world—the rugged Andes. In one small area of these snowcapped peaks live one of the world's largest flying birds and also some of the world's smallest.

Weighing twenty to thirty pounds, with a wing span of eight to ten feet, the *Andean condor* is the largest member of the vulture family and the world's largest bird of prey. Unlike other birds of prey, vultures do not usually hunt. They eat mostly carrion, as well as eggs and fruit. They find their food mostly by sight, although they may also use smell. Eating carrion is a messy business. Condors' bare heads and necks dry quickly in the sun. This helps them keep clean and free from the germs dead animals carry.

If the condors are the giants of flying birds, the *hummingbirds* are the midgets. The jewel-like "hummers" seem too delicate to survive in the Andes, but survive they do. In fact, these nectar-feeding birds pollinate half of the flowering plants there. When they stick their long, thin bills into the flowers, the pollen brushes onto their beaks and is transferred to other flowers at other feedings.

Because hummingbirds get much of their food from hanging flowers on which they cannot perch, they have developed a unique method of flight. They are the only birds that can fly backwards and sideways and hover like helicopters. To hover, they must beat their wings rapidly. This frequent, quick wing beating produces the hum from which the birds get their name.

Marvelous spatule-tail hummingbird

Sword-billed hummingbird

Andean hill star

Andean condor

Lammergeier

Dipper

Mount Everest

The Himalayas of Asia are the world's tallest mountain range. The highest peak among them is Mount Everest. A relative of the condors lives there—the *lammergeier,* or *bearded vulture.*

While the lammergeier will eat the flesh and organs of dead animals, it is the only vulture that also regularly feeds on bones. Known as the "bone-cracker," the bird drops animal bones on rocks to split them. Then it scoops out the marrow with its strong, narrow, grooved tongue. It can also swallow and digest whole bones up to ten inches long. Lammergeiers will drop and eat tortoises as well.

Male and female lammergeiers perform incredible acrobatics in courtship flight. The most dramatic is the "whirling display." In this display the birds lock claws with each other and tumble through the air to within a few yards of the ground.

Another fascinating bird found in both the Andes and the Himalayas is the *dipper,* the only swimming songbird. With stout but unwebbed feet, the dipper dives and swims in fast-flowing mountain streams, searching for larvae, fish eggs, and other food. A well-developed third eyelid protects its vision, and a flap seals off its nostrils when it plunges under the surface. In addition, the dipper's claws enable it to walk underwater to probe weeds and rocks. To keep its feathers waterproof, the dipper has a very large oil gland, ten times the size of other songbirds'.

Oceans

Oceans are the greatest free seafood restaurants on earth. They cater to many diners— whales, porpoises, sea lions, all kinds of fish, and, most certainly, birds. Some birds spend most of their lives at sea, settling on land only to mate and breed. Many fly long distances each year in their search for food or breeding grounds. Among these champion travelers are the *wandering albatross,* the *storm petrel,* and the *arctic tern.*

Found only in the world's southern oceans, the wandering albatross regularly circles the globe. It sometimes covers two hundred and fifty or more miles each day. It is the largest flying seabird and has the longest wings of any bird. On both sea and shore, the albatross has trouble taking off and landing. But once airborne, it is a masterful glider, riding the air currents as it wanders.

The smallest and most abundant seabird, the storm petrel, is found in both of the earth's hemispheres. It migrates between Antarctica, where it

Storm petrel

Wandering albatross

Arctic tern

Red phalarope

ern phalarope

breeds, and the Atlantic Ocean, just short of the Arctic Circle, where it spends the summer. Seagoers are very familiar with this bird, which they often see "water walking"—bounding from wave to wave as if on springs.

Albatrosses and petrels are world-class distance flyers. But the gold medal for longest migration goes to the arctic tern. It travels back and forth between the North and South Poles—a distance of over twenty thousand miles each year.

Far out at sea you do not usually find many wading birds. Two exceptions are the *northern* and *red phalaropes.* Seen on coasts during migration and on arctic islands during breeding, these phalaropes spend the rest of their year swimming in the ocean. To stir up their prey of small crustaceans and larvae, the birds whirl round and round in a circle on the water, sometimes as fast as sixty spins per minute.

Female phalaropes are larger and more colorful than the males. They do the courting, and one female may have several mates. She, of course, lays the eggs, but it is the male or males who raise the young—an unusual arrangement in the bird world.

The Serengeti Plains

Between Africa's forests and deserts lie the great *savannas.* The number and variety of animals who live on these grasslands are remarkable—from the vegetarian elephants and rhinos and the meat-eating lions and leopards to a large concentration of exotic birds.

An unmistakable resident of one of these savannas, the Serengeti Plains in Tanzania, is the long-legged *ostrich.* It is the heaviest and tallest bird in the world. Males can weigh over three hundred pounds and stand over eight feet tall. Although ostriches cannot fly, they can walk tirelessly over great distances and run as fast as forty-five or more miles per hour. They can also kick powerfully with their legs and feet —hard enough to cut open a man's stomach or fracture his skull. But they are much more likely to flee than to attack.

In the grass, ostriches can find plenty to eat. *Flamingos,* on the other hand, find their food in the water. On the Serengeti there are soda lakes, bodies of water filled with salts and other minerals. Although not good for drinking, salt water can provide good eating. The many small organisms in the soda lakes are eaten by the *greater*

Ostrich

Lesser flamingo

Masked weaver

Pin-tailed whydah

Greater honeyguide

and *lesser flamingos.* The birds filter out the food with specialized bills that they sweep upside down in the water. Young flamingos are fed a special milk produced in both parents' *crops*— bag-like parts of the birds' throats. Flamingos, pigeons, and emperor penguins are the only birds known to produce milk.

Among the scattered trees of the Serengeti are some other unique birds. There are *weavers,* which build complex nests that can dangle like scores of lanterns from a single palm tree. Related to the weavers, the *whydahs* do not build nests at all. They *parasitize* other birds. That means they lay their eggs in other birds' nests and let the foster parents raise the whydah chicks as their own.

Another parasitic bird is the *greater honeyguide.* Unlike whydah chicks, which do not harm their foster brothers and sisters, honeyguide chicks kill their nest mates with needle-sharp hooks on their beaks. Then they push the dead bodies out of the nest. When the honeyguides are about ten days old, the hooks fall off.

Adult honeyguides have a much more likeable habit, from which they get their name. They lead *ratels*—honey badgers—and other animals, as well as people, to bees' nests. After the ratel opens the nest for the honey and larvae, the honeyguide eats the rest of the grubs and, oddly enough, the wax, which the bird can digest.

Senegal

In the West African country of Senegal, the lives of numerous birds revolve around the many rivers that flow there and the palms and other trees that grow by these rivers. The *palm-nut vulture* lives in Senegal. It is an unusual vulture because it feeds mostly on oil-palm fruit instead of carrion. The *African palm swift* also inhabits the area. It uses its saliva to fasten little nests of feathers and fibers to the underside of palm leaves and to glue its tiny eggs to the nests.

During the day, the riverbanks are visited by several unusual waders such as the *hammerhead.* It shuffles along in the water to stir up its prey. Hammerhead pairs build the largest roofed nests of any bird. The nests can be three to six and a half feet across and weigh as much as two hundred pounds. No one knows why the birds build such enormous nests—especially since they use the nest for only one season. The next year, the old, abandoned nests are taken over by other birds, snakes, and rats.

At the river's edge, the *Egyptian plover* looks for its insect prey. It will

African palm swift

Hammerhead

Palm-nut vulture

Red-throated bee-eater

White-throated bee-eater

Egyptian plover

Pin-tailed sandgrouse

also, according to some accounts, climb all over crocodiles to remove ticks and other bugs, even going so far as to enter the reptile's mouth to clean its teeth. Egyptian plovers nest right on the ground under the hot sun. Parent birds will bury both eggs and chicks in a light layer of sand to protect them from the heat. The adults will also soak their belly feathers to wet down the eggs, sometimes as often as every few minutes.

The *sandgrouse,* another ground nester, will soak its belly feathers to bring water to its young. Specially structured feathers on the male's stomach absorb the liquid like a sponge. When the bird returns to his chicks, they sip the water from his feathers.

Red-throated and *white-throated bee-eaters* do not nest on the ground. They make their nests in tunnels in the riverbanks. At the end of each tunnel is a chamber where the female lays her eggs. The nest is drilled out by both parent birds and by a group of helpers. Most of these helpers are family members too young to breed. They are also responsible for helping to feed the chicks. Sometimes all of them will roost together in the hole, making it one crowded nest.

Lahore, Pakistan

Many people think the only birds you will find in a city are pigeons and sparrows. But this isn't true. Many different types of birds live in cities. In Lahore, Pakistan, a large and ancient city with two million human inhabitants, live both the *common tailorbird* and the *Indian white-backed vulture.*

One of the best-known birds of the region, the tailorbird makes a unique nest. It first chooses a leaf and punctures it along the edges with its beak. The tailorbird then sews the edges together with thread made of fibers or cobwebs. Inside this envelope or cradle, the bird makes a cup of grass, feathers, wool, or cotton. The outer cradle provides a good disguise and helps keep out the rain. The inner cup cushions the eggs and keeps them warm. There is some variety in tailorbird nests. Sometimes two large leaves are joined, or several smaller ones. But they all show the bird's amazing talent for tailoring.

Dwelling in cities all over southern Asia, Indian white-backed vultures are among Lahore's most reliable scavengers. When the vultures see other scavengers around carrion, they fly down to feed. In some parts of India and Pakistan dead people are not buried or cremated. There these vultures are welcomed as a way of disposing of the bodies. Although their diet may sound disgusting, the birds perform a great service. By ridding the land of decaying carcasses, they help eliminate breeding grounds for bacteria that could harm the living.

Common tailorbird

Indian white-backed vulture

White stork

Jackdaw

Rust, Austria

Not far from the big city of Vienna, Austria, is the smaller town of Rust. There, on nearly every cottage roof, you can see the large platform nests of another city bird—the *white stork.* Migrating distances of over six thousand miles each year, these storks return to these same rooftops every season.

Storks are thought to bring good luck. They were once found breeding all over eastern Europe. Their nests were not only protected but actually kept up by people for centuries. Unfortunately, the birds are much rarer now. Their decline is due both to the draining of the marshes where they feed and to the hunting of the birds themselves.

Nearly voiceless, storks communicate mainly by *bill clapping*—snapping their mandibles together. The sound can be heard for half a mile.

Another bird found in Rust and many other European cities and towns is the *jackdaw,* which is related to the crow. Jackdaws are famous for their love of shiny objects, which they will often steal and add to their nests. Jackdaws take only one mate for life, but the pairs live in colonies that have a strict *pecking order.* That means some birds are the top birds, feeding first and getting the best morsels, while others are lower-ranked and have to wait in line. The lower-ranked birds are kept in their place by pecks from their superiors.

A Rain Forest, Borneo

On the lower slopes of Mount Kinabalu in Borneo, the third largest island in the world, is a rich rain forest. It is known for an astounding variety of birds. Living on the ground is the rare and shy *Argus pheasant.* The male's gorgeous tail—the longest and largest of any bird's—is covered with hundreds of eyespots. When the light strikes them in a certain way the eyespots look three-dimensional. During breeding season, the male shows off his tail during a complex dance he performs in a clearing on the ground. His dance and plumage attract the females, and he will mate with several of them. The hens then leave to raise their chicks alone.

A male *hornbill* has only one mate, and during breeding season he must care for her in an extraordinary way. After the female lays her eggs in a tree-hole nest, she plasters up the hole from the inside with her droppings, saliva, fruit pulp, and lumps of mud. The male must feed the female through a small slit while she incubates the

Great argus
pheasant

Edible nest swiftlet

hornbill

eggs. Later, after they hatch, he feeds both her and the chicks for some weeks. Then the female breaks out and the young replaster the hole. Both parents now feed them until they break out and fly away.

There are a number of different hornbills in Africa and Asia. In this Borneo rain forest, common species include the *rhinoceros, wreathed,* and *helmeted hornbills.* All have huge bills generally topped by a horny growth called a *casque.* Although the bills look heavy, they are actually a lightweight honeycomb of bony tissue. The one exception is the helmeted hornbill's. Its casque is solid ivory. Unfortunately, the

bird has been heavily hunted for this ivory, as well as for its extra-long tail feathers.

The *edible nest swiftlets* that live in Mount Kinabalu's caves are not hunted. But their nests are. Made of saliva, and sometimes other materials, the nests are harvested by the millions for soup. The caves that the swiftlets inhabit are very dark. To fly through them without crashing into the walls, the swiftlets make a series of high-pitched sounds that bounce off the walls and back to their ears. This sonar system is called *echolocation* and is similar to the one employed by bats.

A Rain Forest, Papua New Guinea

A remote and wild island rarely visited by tourists, Papua New Guinea is covered by thick rain forests. About seven hundred species of birds live there—three times as many types of birds as mammals. In this paradise for birds, what else would you expect to find but *birds of paradise?*

Birds of paradise are among the most spectacularly plumed of all birds. Like some of the other colorful species introduced in this book, the males are generally the ones with the dramatic feathers. And they show off their plumage in dazzling displays to attract mates.

The *magnificent bird of paradise* alone performs several displays. For the most complex one, he clears twigs and leaves from a stage or arena on the ground. Then he strips the leaves from a young tree within or overhanging the arena. While the female watches, he dances up and down the tree with his neck and back feathers raised to form a cape, his breast feathers vibrating, tail wires quivering, and head bobbing from side to side.

Magnificent
bird of paradise

Macgregor's
gardenerbird

The plainer *bowerbirds* are related to the striking birds of paradise. Male bowerbirds have developed a different and truly remarkable way to attract females. They build *bowers.* The bowers range from simple cleared spaces decorated with mats of leaves and twigs to extraordinary structures that resemble huts or avenues. Bowerbirds are the only birds to build elaborate constructions that are not nests. Some bowerbirds will actually paint their bowers. For brushes, they use shreds of bark or leaves; and for paint, fruit pulp, grass, or charcoal mixed with saliva.

In this forest, the *Macgregor's gardenerbird,* a type of bowerbird, builds a tower bower. Around a small tree, the male piles sticks and twigs, breaking off the tips so that they are of equal length. He covers them with moss and also places moss in a circle on the ground. He decorates both the circle and the tower with black, orange-brown, and yellow objects such as seeds, fruit, leaves, charcoal, and bits of insects. As many as five hundred decorations can be found in one gardenerbird's bower. And no two bowers are ever alike. After he completes the bower, the gardenerbird will sing and dance and display his orange crest to lure a female. After they mate, she alone will build the nest and raise the young.

New Zealand

In the western South Pacific lies New Zealand, a country made up of two large islands and several smaller ones. Far away from other big bodies of land, New Zealand once had only two types of mammals—both bats—but many native birds. Huge flightless *moas* lived there until they were hunted to extinction. Today several kinds of flightless birds still roam the forests, but they are seriously endangered. Introduced mammals and other birds have hurt the native birds by preying on them, spreading disease, or taking over their habitats. The destruction of their forests to make grazing land has also caused the birds' decline.

One of the rarest birds is the *kakapo,* the world's heaviest parrot and the only one that cannot fly. It is, however, a good climber. Called the "owl parrot" because of its owl-like facial discs, the kakapo lives in holes around tree roots. It comes out at night to feed on grasses and leaves. Male kakapos put on an unusual courtship display. They dig

Kakapo

Kea

Brown kiwi

several bowls in the ground in one big area. Then each male gets into a bowl and makes a booming call. The kakapo makes its boom with an inflatable sac in his chest.

A symbol of New Zealand found on stamps and posters is the *kiwi.* It is another flightless native bird that has declined in number, although not as severely as the kakapo. Like the parrot, the kiwi stays in its burrow near tree roots during the day. At night it emerges to find worms, insects, and fruit on the forest floor. The kiwi has poor eyesight but a good sense of smell. Unlike other birds, it has nostrils at the tip of its beak. Both kiwis and kakapos also have whiskers around their bills to help them find their food.

A more abundant New Zealand bird is another parrot—the *kea.* Nesting in rock tunnels and tree trunks in the mountains, the kea is the only parrot that lives where there is snow. Unlike other parrots, the kea is not a vegetarian. It will eat many types of food, including carrion. It has also been known to fly down chimneys into peoples' homes in search of a meal.

Australia, the Mallee

An island, a country, a continent, Australia is a land of extremes—from high mountains to flat deserts, from tall tropical rain forests to areas of dwarf eucalyptus trees called the *mallee.* Found in southern and central Australia, these scrubby woodlands are where *mallee fowl* make their home.

Mallee fowl do not incubate their eggs by sitting on them. Instead, they build huge mounds of sand and leaves. As the leaves decay they incubate the eggs laid inside the mound. The temperature inside the nest must be kept at around ninety-one degrees, so the male constantly tests it with his mouth lining and tongue. To adjust the temperature, he will open up the mound or add more sand. Because of the long breeding period, each male mallee fowl may tend the mound for up to eleven months of the year. When the chicks hatch, they have to struggle up out of the mound and then care for themselves without their parents' help.

Budgeriger

Rainbow lorikeet

Mallee fowl

Sulfur-crested cockatoos

Emu

A common bird living in the mallee is the *emu.* Five feet tall and flightless, the emu is a relative of the ostrich. Male ostriches court females. But among emus, it is the females who do the courting, while the males raise the young.

Also abundant in the mallee are many parrots. There are about fifty species of parrots throughout Australia. Nearly all of the world's *cockatoos* are native to this country. Cockatoos are known for their lovely crests and their loud voices. Like other parrots, they are famous for their ability to imitate human speech and also for their longevity. One *sulfur-crested cockatoo* lived over eighty years in captivity. Cockatoos travel in pairs and flocks. Each flock has a *sentinel,* or guard. When the birds feed on the ground, the sentinel perches in a tree. If a predator appears, the sentinel shrieks an alarm and the whole flock flies away.

Lorikeets and *lories* live in the mallee and the rain forests. They crush flowers and soak up nectar and pollen with their brush-tipped tongues. *Budgerigars* are the most abundant of all Australian parrots. They wander in great flocks all over the country. Commonly called parakeets, they are the best-known parrots in the world.

Antarctica

Great skua

No place on earth is as cold as Antarctica. Most of the land is permanently covered with ice. The wind blows harshly. In winter, temperatures can drop to over seventy-five degrees below zero. The only plants found are algae, lichens, and mosses. The only native animals found on the land—or the ice— are seals and birds. Most of those birds are the flightless, fish-eating penguins.

In the chilly antarctic spring, *Adélie penguins* trek miles and miles from the sea across the ice to their coastal breeding areas. They may walk, or "toboggan," across the ice on their plump bellies. The males come first to stake out their territory. The females follow and pair up with their mates. Because there are no leaves or branches to be found, they build nests of small stones on the bare ground.

Adélie penguin chicks have a few persistent enemies. At sea, there is the leopard seal. On land, the chief predator is the *great skua*. This gull-like bird eats Adélie chicks. It is also the only bird that breeds at both the North and South Poles. Each pole has a different population of skuas, and they do not migrate.

Adélie penguin

Emperor
penguin

The Adélies leave during the fall to spend the winter at sea, often floating on the ice floes. As their breeding season ends, the *emperor penguins'* season begins. Emperors are the largest of all penguins—three to four feet tall and weighing sixty to one hundred pounds. They hold the record for the deepest dive—nearly nine hundred feet underwater—as well as the longest—eighteen minutes. They are also the only birds in the world to breed during the antarctic winter. Like other penguins, they are protected from the cold by insulating layers of feathers and fat. Penguins molt all their feathers at once, the new ones pushing out the old.

Emperors don't build nests. As soon as the female lays her single egg, the male scoops it onto his feet and covers it with a loose flap of belly skin. For two months the males sit there while the females feed at sea. The mothers return just as the chicks hatch. By then the fathers, who have not eaten, have lost as much as half their weight. They head out to sea to feed as the females take charge of the young.

When the winter ends, all the emperors depart. Then the Adélies return and the cycle begins again.

Index

About the Author

Marilyn Singer is the author of numerous books for children, including novels, nonfiction, and poetry. *Turtle in July,* illustrated by Jerry Pinkney, was an American Library Association Notable Book and a *Booklist* Editor's Choice selection. Ms. Singer is herself an avid birder. She and her husband live in Brooklyn with a collection of birds, cats, and a dog.

About the Illustrator

James Needham studied art at the California College of Arts and Crafts in Oakland, California, and at Pratt Institute in Brooklyn, New York. He is now a free-lance illustrator and fine artist with a special interest in nature. He now lives in Colorado Springs, Colorado, at the foot of Pikes Peak with his wife and many animal friends.

The Pribilof Islands

The Atlantic Coast

The Sonoran Desert

The Galápagos Islands

The Everglades

Senegal

Rain Forest, Peru

The Andes Mountains

Antarctica